EMOTIONAL
Ramblings

JACINTA HUDSON

Copyright © October 2020 Jacinta Hudson

All rights reserved. No part of this book may be reproduced without the written consent of the copyright holder except in the case of quotations for a book review.

Cover Design by Stone Ridge Books

ISBN: 978-0-6489289-0-4

To Jensen
My dream come true.

As you read the lines, you watch it all play out.
You know it all too well, even though it's not your story.
The voice rings loud and true, the feelings seem so real.
Like you were living out the plot.
The pain, fear, love, and glory.

Putting the book down, you take in your surroundings.
It hits too close to home; you need a break from the intensity.
How could these words describe your life?
You've never met the author.
Either way, I've just inspired you, to try writing.
Just like me.

JACINTA HUDSON

❦

My breath catches. My heart races.
My mind stops. My stomach sinks.
The sound of an angel. Or possibly the devil.
My world starts to crumble. This stinks.

❦

Who needs to make a wise choice?
You're only making a life choice.
It's not as if this choice could change your world.
Who needs to make a smart decision,
When there's more than one person a part of the decision?
In deciding who I want within my world.

I know that you're not mine,
But you're always on my mind.
I know you're with another,
But the thought, it makes me shudder.

Rose petals are soft,
But their thorns are rather sharp.
Just like they cut your fingers,
That's how you broke my heart.

JACINTA HUDSON

❧

The sun is bright, but there's stress inside.
Opportunities surround me, while butterflies fly within me.
My stomach churns as my emotions turn.
I'm waiting for my turn, though I know my time is here.
Here and now, and all around me.
The waves are crashing on my moment.
I just have to stand up and take it.

❧

The future is fast, and it scares me.
It passes in the blink of an eye.
It comes and it goes,
And god only knows,
If I'll catch a moment before it flies by.

EMOTIONAL RAMBLINGS

❧

The idea of something different.
The excitement of something new.
The thrill of something breathtaking.
And the longing for it too.

The best part about new beginnings
Is the fresh start for those involved.
And the happiness that spreads throughout
The place that has evolved.

JACINTA HUDSON

☙❧

You tell me that I'm beautiful.
That I'm sweet and smart and kind.
And then you tell me I've got it all wrong.
Have you lost your bloody mind?!

☙❧

I worry about your family.
I fear for your sanity.
I tear up over your reality.
I wish for you, serenity.

I love you wholeheartedly.
I want to hold you close to me.
And show you what I see.
In you is strength and beauty.

EMOTIONAL RAMBLINGS

"I can't lose another person."
I can't bear to stand your pain.
I've had more than my share of losses.
People falling like the rain.

You tell me to "Get over it".
There's something you don't know.
While I'm acting sympathetic.
I'm only putting on a show.

You can be so narrow minded.
You can only see your side.
Telling others to keep on fighting.
When all you want to do is hide.

I can see your inner strength.
Shining bright from deep within you.
I just wish you would believe me.
And let it come shining through.

"You should know that I'm still your friend."
The words that go 'round in my head.
"If you ever have any doubt, just know that hasn't changed.
"I'll always be there in the end."

A breath of fresh air as the words reach my ear.
Even in doubt, I always knew it to be true.
To be expected, after all these years, I always knew the real you.
But that doesn't mean it isn't comforting to hear.

It's good to know I've got you,
Through thick and thin, no matter what.
To lean on. To rely on. To trust that you'll be there.
But then, nothing's changed. I always knew you cared.

EMOTIONAL RAMBLINGS

☙❧

You seem a little lost inside. Like you don't know who you are.
I hope you know that you can confide, in me if you need.
If you've got pain you need to share, then I will help you out.
Because I'm not going anywhere. Baby I've got your back.

☙❧

Roses are bold.
Violets are cold.
Even though I love you
It's time to start anew.

JACINTA HUDSON

❦

All I need is a place to breathe.
A tiny place for me to live.
But you don't care for what I want or need.
A small space is too much to give.

❦

I'm quiet lately and you've noticed.
I don't really know what to say.
I'm trying to pretend, like there's nothing going on in my head.
But I'm yet to have found the right way.

❧

The move that makes you happy,
Is the same one that terrifies me.
The one change that traps me in ambiguity,
Is the one that sets you free.

❧

1234, I declare a romantic war.
5678, Please don't break my heart today.

1234, I wish we could be so much more.
5678, But I'm afraid I've left it far too late.

JACINTA HUDSON

❧

I don't know how I feel about you today.
And I don't know what it is I want to say.
But I know that I miss you, and I know that I love you.
And I know that everything will be ok.

❧

My neck hurts but I'm happy.
My head hurts but I'm glad.
My heart hurts but I'm moving forward.
Away from something bad.

There's a light in you.
Can you feel it?
Can you see it?
Do you know it's shining through?

It's the kind that tells the truth.
We can hear it.
Screaming at us.
But it seems ever dim to you.

For the moment you can't see.
But one day you'll be blinded.
By the brightness of the light in you.
That shines through, loud and true.

JACINTA HUDSON

In a world of ugly faces,
I am beautiful.
In a world of senseless twits,
I am wise.
In a world of egocentric pricks,
I am selfless.
In a world of twisted haters,
I love with all my heart.

In a world with trashy tabloids,
I am talented.
In a world with no emotion,
I will cry.
In a world of social media,
I will endeavour to call my friends.
In a world of blind denial,
I will continue to ask "why?"

❧

Take a deep breath and jump off the ledge.
Take a deep breath Take the plunge.
Life's only worth living if you live on the edge.
Life's only worth living if you live it.
Take a step forward; put a skip in your step.
Take a step forward, toward your future.
The world will keep going long after you're gone.
So, make an impression while you're here.

❧

Pain. Strain. Ache. Chill.
I've yet to figure out my path, but I know I will.
Calm. Still. Warm. Relaxed.
That side of me has been missing,
But I know she's coming back.

JACINTA HUDSON

❧

Lier, Lier, pants on fire.
Drove the car and burnt the tyres.
Went round the town handing out the flyers.
All the while, being a Lier, Lier, Lier.

❧

Thoughts unfinished.
Like words unsaid.
And actions left undone.
Questions and answers
Leave a mess in my head.
And I can't tell what's right and what's wrong.

EMOTIONAL RAMBLINGS

Bombshells and curveballs keep me reeling.
You've got me questioning everything I'm feeling.
I don't know what I want, or how I want to get it.
I don't know what my next step is,
but I know I won't forget it.

If "one door closes, another will open",
then I think we've blown a wall out.
I want to try taking risks,
but I'm not ready to deal with the fall out.

I need to find some clarity,
find my head and follow my heart.
I need to start making decisions,
but I don't know where to start.

JACINTA HUDSON

Pen to paper in my bedroom,
Trying to make sense of it all.
I break it down and scribble it out
And throw paper against the wall.

It's a stanza from a poem,
Or the chorus of a song.
Like the moment when your eyes meet across the room
And you can't speak.

When it feels like a dream until you blink.
A pinch and now I'm wide awake.

EMOTIONAL RAMBLINGS

☙❧

Pregnancy. Hay fever. Allergies and such.
The endless opinions that bug me so much.
Headaches. Back strain. The pain in my neck.
I think it's time you got your attitude checked.

☙❧

Smooth. Deep. Beautiful.
Exciting. Scary. Trouble.
Pure. Whole. Rich.
Morally bankrupt Bitch.

JACINTA HUDSON

༒

Your touch so soft.
Your tongue so warm.
Your body next to mine.

Your stubble rough.
Your passion hot.
Your arms that hold me tight.

You're completely different
From the men I usually fall for.
The moment I first saw you,
I watched my jaw drop to the floor.
And since that moment I've been hooked.
You never stop surprising me.
I can't remember the last time I felt this way.
I've developed a crush, and I'm intrigued.

JACINTA HUDSON

☙❧

I can't picture my life without you.
But that's what I'm trying to do.
I'm trying to imagine a life without the passion.
I will one day find within you.

☙❧

My mind is foggy, and my heart is heavy.
It's all too much today.
My life got busy and I'm not quite ready.
But I haven't the time to delay.

EMOTIONAL RAMBLINGS

Do you ever have the feeling,
When you know you're falling down?
When your roots have been uplifted,
And your branches hit the ground.

You can't tell land from sky,
As your heart begins to pound.
Then you try to find your balance,
But you just turn round and round.

You feel the tug upon you,
As the gravity wins out.
The numbness is painful agony,
But you haven't the strength to shout.

JACINTA HUDSON

≈≈

I pull the cover over my head.
It doesn't change the dim inside.
The darkness crept in many years ago.
I've got plaster by the gallons.
But I can't keep up with the cracking.
As the pressure breaks the dam I've come to know.

Water gushes through the hole.
The coming flood is daunting.
For all I know is I will surely drown.
Liquid pours into my lungs.
I can't breathe, my arms are flailing.
As to the depths of darkness I am bound.

※

The weight of you is too much to bear.
The darkness surrounds me everywhere.
I can't breathe these fumes that hang in the air.
It's heavy on my chest and I'm scared.

※

A breath to stop the shaking.
An image to calm me down.
For I must stay upward facing.
Or, under anxiety, I'll drown.

JACINTA HUDSON

❧

The colours I see are all fleeting.
They fly by the eye of my mind.
Each one is a symbol with meaning.
A melody untethered by time.

Brown keeps me grounded when I'm floating.
Green is the sign of new life.
Red throws me deep into passion.
And as equally deep into strife.

Blue is as soft as is bold.
But both shades keep me cool, calm, collected.
But orange and purple have me sold.
Sparking a feeling that must be protected.

Pink hangs with yellow in the bright summer sun.
Black paints the background they're all framed in.
White is as bright as my strive to have fun.
Silver lines the clouds from within

❧

Hope comes in the form of flowers,
The promise of the spring ahead.
Faith comes in the form of grace,
The belief that one is not mislead.
Love comes in the form of smiles,
The comfort in the words unsaid.
Life comes in the form of dreams,
The desires conjured up in bed.

❧

Fairy-tale princes have flowy hair.
And real ones have it slicked back.
Fairy-tale princes fight and dare.
Where real ones like to kick back.
Fairy-tale princesses are shabby chic.
But real ones are always high street.
Fairy-tale princesses are locked away,
So, the real ones are clearly better to meet..

JACINTA HUDSON

The pen is mightier than the sword
And your words are daggers in me.
They cut to insecurities
That no one else can harm.
No need for repetition,
We've heard the joke before.
No need for one more insult.
Isn't it time we closed this door?
Do you really think so little of me?
Is it so hard for you to care?
Why can't you see it from my side?
Is what I'm asking so unfair?
You know it hurts me every time,
But you still come back again.
Is it my tears that you're addicted to?
Or do you just long to see my pain?
Something that always amazes me,
I don't mind being alone,
But the scary thought inside of me-
The occasional dread of coming home.

Now that the pain is slowly subsiding,
All I feel like doing is crying.
The break in my heart. The knife in my back.
The stress for a part of my life that I lack.
Worked to the bone, my brain is aching.
I feel the weight in every decision I'm making.

A rickety bridge is before me,
I can't tell if it's safe from this side.
But I've got to make a move, to move forward.
And it's not as though from life I can hide.

Reaching for you is like reaching for true love,
reaching for new love,
exciting and scary.

Reaching for you is worth all the fear love,
it's worth it for you love,
this I promise is true.

It might take me a while to get to my true love,
to get close to you love,
but I swear that I will.

For nothing will stop me from chasing that new love,
from finding my true love,
from getting to you.

※

A beautiful blessing. A wonderful thing.
And I can't wait to hold you in my arms.
A spectacular blessing. A marvellous thing.
And I know your family will be around,
To keep you safe from harm.

※

With the world at my feet. All the people that I meet.
Every breath that I breathe. And I'm happy.
At the start of a life, where I'm a mother and a wife.
And I'll push past all the strife, to be happy.

JACINTA HUDSON

The beat in my heart, it falters.
I choke back the pain in my tears.
My gut is wrenched out. The salt reaches my mouth.
As reality catches up with my fears.

The words of your knife cut my skin.
Turns out, the text is mightier than the pen.
The harsh light of day, fades, as the sun goes away.
And I'm left in the dark, like back when.

The silence is blaring in my ears.
I can't quite feel the cold.
The walls are caving in. I find I'm trapped within.
As to the darkness, I am called.

Pain stabs into my heart, but I can't feel it.
There's a life before my eyes, but I can't see it.
A voice screams in my head, but I can't hear it.
I know there's a way out, but I can't reach it.

§

I've wanted you forever.
And now that you're so near,
I want to run in the other direction.
Who the hell invented fear?

JACINTA HUDSON

❧

Bless you on your wedding day.
Forever you will be
Joined on such a blessed day.
Together you'll be free.

❧

When your world falls apart and you feel all alone,
You will always have someone to turn to.
And when you're doubting yourself
and you don't know what's right.
You'll always have someone to tell you the truth.
Because your best friend's your lover,
and you know there'll be no other,
Who will love you the way that they do.

❧

A love like yours is like no other.
It's not like the love you have for your mother.
Or your brother.
Or your sister.
Or your father.
Or your friend.
A love like yours stays strong until the end.

❧

The smile in your eyes says it all.
You met the one person who could change your whole world.
You're brighter and lighter and happier too.
And we've not doubt it'll be "Always & Forever" for you.

JACINTA HUDSON

You ask me if I'm ok.
I tell you that I'm fine.
We both know that I'm lying.
But I won't change my mind.

You'll pat me on the shoulder,
And gently kiss my head.
You'll be an ear when I need you here.
But I'd rather be alone instead.

Because breaking down and talking it out
Won't fix this hole inside.
There's only one thing that could cure it.
The thing that clouds my heart and mind.

You'll ask me if I'm ok.
And I'll tell you that I'm fine.
We both know that's not true,
But there's nothing you can do.
I just need a little time.

EMOTIONAL RAMBLINGS

❧

I can see that my whole world is changing.
And I don't know if you see it too.
You're looking left and right,
But you don't have my sight.
I'm looking straight down the centre too.

❧

Not ready to move forward,
But so sick of looking back.
All I really want from you,
Is to know that you won't hurt me.

Not yet ready to move forward,
But so tired of looking back.
I'm fighting fear inside you know.
Will you help me to break free?

JACINTA HUDSON

❧

The kindest of smiles, the sweetest of hearts.
A new face on the scene of my ever-crazy movie.
The gentlest of hugs, the softest of words.
But this is a drama, and it's never that easy.

Excited at first, and then fear sets in.
I'm flattered, and honoured, and I want to get to know you.
Then reality sets in and I remember my heart,
It belongs to another, and I don't know how to tell you.

I could be overreacting; you might take it very well.
Or I could back away right now, and just save us both the hell.

EMOTIONAL RAMBLINGS

❧

The building is on fire and I've got a burning question.
Now please don't be a liar, as I ask what's on my mind.

If a person tries to save another,
while the second tries to save the other.
Will either make it out alive,
or will we both burn together inside?

JACINTA HUDSON

In all of your obscurities
All I see are purities.
Those traits that you abhor,
Are the ones that I adore.

Your uniqueness is alarming.
Yet I find it rather charming.
There's something different about you.
And it comes across real and true.

I don't regret a thing.
The good. The bad. The ugly. The pain I held within.
I don't regret the choices I made.
I made my bed, and that's where I laid.
I don't regret the things I said.
I only spoke those I knew true.
Nor do I regret the things I did.
Each my own choice, my hand was never forced by you.
I do not regret the way it played out.
For, every hill will make me climb.
I do not regret the ache in my heart.
As I know that one day, I will find what is mine.

JACINTA HUDSON

꙰

Many years after we thought we'd lose you,
You stayed to keep us company.
And while distance grew between us,
I've many beautiful moments to remember.

And now it's time to say goodbye,
It's going to be hard to leave you.
You've been a bundle of love from the start,
And I'll keep you in my heart forever.

EMOTIONAL RAMBLINGS

෧෨

Every second is a tic.
Every heartbeat is a tock.
It's the deafening sound.
Of a great grandfather clock.

It is quiet for the most part.
Until it chimes within my ears.
It rings in my head and stops my heart.
And has been doing so for years.

JACINTA HUDSON

❦

How am I meant to not think about
What has plagued my mind for ten years?
How am I meant to ignore
The single cause of so many tears?

How am I meant to move past
All of the doubts and the fears?
And get to a place of serenity,
Without thinking about you, my dear.

EMOTIONAL RAMBLINGS

☙❧

The weight of the world on your shoulders,
Is heavy, like the head with the crown.
The shape and the size of your ego,
Is twisted, like the ever-sad clown.

Few and far between are your thoughts,
Of anyone else but yourself.
But remember, when travelling alone,
Beside you, you'll find no one else.

JACINTA HUDSON

❦

For every opportunity
There's bound to be a choice
To be heard above the haters,
You'll need to raise your voice.

For every moment in your life,
There's something you can learn.
And to get this moment right,
You must step up and take your turn.

EMOTIONAL RAMBLINGS

≈

Don't fear failure,
For I will hold your hand.
Never fear the loneliness,
For you don't need a man.

≈

Roses are red.
Violets are blue.
Your cooking is yummy.
And so are you.

JACINTA HUDSON

How do you open up?
When you find someone who you can trust.
How do you let them in?
To show them the world that you live in.
How do you share your world?
How do you bare your heart and soul?
How do you let them in?
To the world that you live in.
I've never been any good.
At opening up and letting them in.
I've never been any good.
At trusting that they really care for me.
That they'll be there for me.
So how do you open up?
How do you let go?
How do you release, and let your feelings show?
How do you learn to trust?
How do you open up?

50/50 chance.
Do you know what you would choose?
Left or right? Up or down?
Inside-out? Turned around?

Close your eyes. Can you see me?
Cover your ears. Can you hear me?
Open your heart. Do you want me?
Can you tell me; do you know what's right?

Do you follow your heart or your head?
Do you pray before you go to bed?

Open your eyes. Uncover your ears.
And, should you open your heart and arms for me,
And wrap me in them warmly,
Would you hold me there for years?

JACINTA HUDSON

❧❧

There's a sadistic little bitch in me.
But I keep her locked up tight.
So instead of screwing with your mind all day,
She screws with mine all night.

❧❧

If an image is worth a thousand words,
Then there's no way to paint this picture.
So please tell me, what an emotion is worth,
For I can't see it clearly enough.

EMOTIONAL RAMBLINGS

୨୧

So, because you're older you don't have to respect me.
But I have to show respect to you.
And because you pay rent, you're allowed an opinion.
But there's no way I get to have one too.

It seems that,
Because there's similarities between us.
You appear to know exactly what I should do.
If only you, in all your wisdom, could figure out.
The things I thought I already knew.

JACINTA HUDSON

If I don't show it, you don't know it,
Yet even if I do, you haven't got a clue.
If it's not spoken, you stay un-woken,
Yet spoken loud and true, you still haven't got a clue.

In front of your face, a saving grace,
Just waiting for you to catch up.
But you're blind to see your naivety,
And so, you will never match up
To what the world expects of you.
It's not so hard to say and do,
The few things that we ask of you.

But you haven't got a clue.

EMOTIONAL RAMBLINGS

☙❧

Gotta love how life pushes you down,
Even though you just spent months
Trying to get back up again.

Over life always beating you down?
Very hard to keep on fighting?
Every day, it's so hard to find the strength.
Right looks like wrong, and there's no silver lining.

Interesting point to consider...
Toughen up and move on.

❧

You're drowning in emotion.
So, it's hard for you to see.
The heaviness that you don't like.
Is the same in you and me.

❧

I live a life of pure imagination.
True to my heart are the images I feel.
The problem therein lies that I can't tell the difference.
Between the tales that I dream up,
and the stories that are real.

EMOTIONAL RAMBLINGS

❧

Problems with your lover.
So, you moved on to the next.
But that one didn't work for you,
So, you tried to do what's best.

Problems with another.
But it seems you're in a rut.
As that one didn't work for you.
No one ever makes the cut.

Women are confusing.
Women make things complicated.
Women are the cause it seams
For the problems that you have.

Men like to blame their lover,
And then move on to another.
But did you ever think that maybe,
You cause the problems that you have.

JACINTA HUDSON

❧

I can still see it.
Your eyes looking up at me.
I can still see it.
The smile that got through to me.
And I can still feel it.
Your arms wrapped around me.
I can still see it.
I'm wide awake, but I feel like I'm dreaming.

I know that this is dorky,
But this is who I am.
But who I am is missing something.
I'm looking for a man.
While this is very scary,
It's an adventure I'll trek through.
To see if I can find,
What I'm looking for in you.

JACINTA HUDSON

❧❧

You know how to get to the one thing I can't find.
And you know how to steady the chaos in my mind.
I don't know how you do it, it's difficult for me.
But when I lay beside you, I could float away, I'm free.

❧❧

To think that just five years ago,
It was so very hard to like you.
And now I can't stop smiling.
You've become the man I always knew.

I took a chance on you because I knew I had to.
And I don't regret it for one minute.
I took a risk because I knew I wanted this.
And I wouldn't change one bit.

I hope you take a chance on someone.
When you find The One.
And risk all of it, for the sake of it.
And don't regret a thing.

JACINTA HUDSON

Writers block at the worst of times.
Finding it hard to make words rhyme.
I guess it's not a tragedy.
It's not the words, but what they mean to me,
That's important to the story line.
I guess these ones will do,
I suppose that they are fine.

The silence is golden.
The stillness is sweet.
In no other moment,
Would I rather be.

There's no noise around me.
There isn't a sound.
At this time of night,
When there's no one around.

JACINTA HUDSON

You don't notice that you need me,
Until the moment that you do.
You spend hours looking for blu tack,
When what you really need is glue.

You know that I'm the best you've got,
And you know that you would miss me.
But you tend to forget this little fact,
While you're cracking a little hissy.

EMOTIONAL RAMBLINGS

☙❧

When the rain is falling down and the sun's gone into hiding.
When there's no one else around and you're standing all alone.
That's the time to do the stupid things.
So, grab a ladder and start climbing.
Just hope you don't fall down when you're standing all alone.

☙❧

Why is it that I fear the darkness,
When I turn out the light?
But when the power blows all on its own,
I'm calm throughout the night?

Another line. Another step.
Another song. Another poem.
Another change in my direction.
I never know just where I'm going.

Another word. Another turn.
Another note. Another drawing.
How can I take my next step,
When I can't get my footing?

Another place. Another face.
Another dress. Another smile.
After years of looking one way.
I feel it's taken me a while.

Another name. Another game.
Another life. Another light.
Now I see the bigger picture.
It's time to finally do what's right.

What if what I know, I don't?
And what is real just isn't?
And what if all I think I am,
I've never really been?

What if all my friends, just aren't?
And what if what I like, I don't?
And what if the things I say I'll do,
It turns out that I won't?

What if my life is upside down?
What if I'm topsy turvy?
What if the life I'm living now,
Was never meant to be this way?

What if I figure out the answers?
What will become of me then?
Will I have to change everything I am?
Or will everything stay the same?

JACINTA HUDSON

Think about yourself, for the sake of all the others,
Who love you, ever so dearly, each and every day.
For, without you, you have to know, their life is incomplete,
And they will carry that pain with them, each and every day.

So, care for your health and your attitude,
and the way you live your life,
And be the best you can be, each and every day.

And be present in their life, and in yours, in every way you can,
No matter what will come your way.
Each and every day.

EMOTIONAL RAMBLINGS

☙❧

You make a plan, and then life turns around,
And changes everything.
Sure of how it will go, but you just never know,
What your life will bring.

As quick as your fingers can snap, or your hands can clap,
In your ears, reality rings.
Everything feels strange, as all your plans change,
And this reality really stings.

JACINTA HUDSON

I miss you every day,
And I know that you know it.
There's nothing much to say,
I want you all the time.

Out in the open, or to myself,
There's always a way to show it.
No need to say a word,
Because the whole world knows you're mine.

EMOTIONAL RAMBLINGS

☙❧

Pictures circling in my mind. Bright colours on the canvas.
A story told with images; of the man I've learned to love.

Singing with your sister, joking with your bro.
Keeping your niece rugged up warm and tight.
It turns out you're a family man. Now, there's the man I love.

You're talented and sexy. I never knew you played guitar.
After years you still surprise me. I guess that's what I love.

The way you look into my eyes.
Your arms around me when it's cold at night.
I've an amazing man in my sights.
And I can't help but falling in love.

JACINTA HUDSON

This little poem is written for you.
Yes, you in the back, who doesn't know what to do.
For the outspoken diva, who's too shy to speak.
For the wild party animal, who's mild mannered and meek.

For those with a voice that don't want to be heard.
Who are happy to skip first place and settle for third.
For the confident souls who would much rather hide.
Passing up the outdoors to stay safely inside.

EMOTIONAL RAMBLINGS

೭⊷ട

Hush my darling, don't you fret, for you are not alone.
The worries that you speak of, it seems, have found their home.

My ears can hear the humming; my eyes are blurry too.
My mind is overcrowded, but they're all listening to you.

So, take your time and ponder, and take your time to feel.
For I need my heart to get me through.
And, in case I hurt, to heal.

JACINTA HUDSON

❧

My words don't make any sense,
And my heart can't make up its mind.
My thoughts are all over the fence.
My head doesn't know how to feel.

❧

Someone else's man is clouding up my dreams.
Even though I know that it can't be.
Someone else's man is on my mind.
And while I've no illusions, I hear his voice with every line.

EMOTIONAL RAMBLINGS

The pain and the exhaustion.
The anxiety and fear.
A move toward a future,
That's so far and yet so near.

I must remind myself at times,
That I'm doing this for the right reasons.
And take a breath, and keep my head,
When I get overwhelmed by feelings.

JACINTA HUDSON

❦

Blue meets blue. The sky is clear.
I hear the waves crashing, but I feel no fear.
The breeze blows lightly, branches on trees sway.
The sun is out, I'm smiling, what a lovely, beautiful day.

❦

Deep breath in. Deep breath out.
It's time to push the pain aside,
And wipe away that pout.

EMOTIONAL RAMBLINGS

❦

The moment that I realised was the moment my life changed.
No way I can go backwards, so I take a giant leap.
I pull up out the front and I can't believe I'm doing this.
My heart is pounding in my chest, as up the path I creep.

The little speech that I've rehearsed, to help me calm my nerves,
Goes flying out the window, so I'm standing still and speechless.
A chill runs up my spine and I'm quaking in my boots here.
I open up my mouth to speak and find that I am breathless.

You're looking at me waiting and I know I'm only wasting time.
My heart says now or never but my mind has left the building.
I gather up my courage and tell you what I'm thinking.
I sigh relief, the deed is done, and now you know my feelings.

JACINTA HUDSON

❧

I can't believe the nerve of you.
In all the things you say and do.
Your attitude is truly so despicable.

You're selfish and narrow minded.
Yet you act as though you're so kind.
To think like that is truly unbelievable.

Your attitude's obnoxious.
Your face just ain't that cute.
Your subtly is drowning me.
You don't know the point is moot.

I'm saying no but you're not listening.
Your ignorance has you blindfolded.
Flattery will get you nowhere.
Take the hint; I'm just not interested.

JACINTA HUDSON

I feel so selfish.
Is it too much to ask for the things that you want?
I feel so heartless.
Are you a horrible person, if what you want keeps others at bay?
I feel so confused.
Do I follow my head or heart on this,
if I can ever decide on the difference?
I feel so lost.
It's almost like, to make a choice,
I have to push something away.

EMOTIONAL RAMBLINGS

Taking baby steps while leaping.
Staying wide awake while sleeping.
Deep breathing when I can't breathe.
With no time to stop and sigh.

Doing circles to get direction.
Making mistakes to find perfection.
Working hard to catch a break.
Feeling low while on a high.

JACINTA HUDSON

❦

The pen twirls in my hand.
I don't know what to write.
While the words twirl in my head,
Because I can't tell wrong from right.

❦

Silence and stillness are usually a good thing.
But today they just drown me in noise.
I don't know what's worse, the pain or the numbness.
And I can't wait to hear your voice.

EMOTIONAL RAMBLINGS

☙❧

One step forward and I can't breathe.
Two steps forward and I can't see.
Another step and now I'm leaping.
I'm too far under and I feel like I'm sinking.

Where's the line between ambition and submission?
Between what you want to do,
and what others expect of you?
What's the difference between fighting for a life,
and fighting for survival?
In a world of corrupt manipulation,
how can you tell a friend from a rival?

If your peers are there to help you through,
But the help you need is to do better than them, do you?
Even if it means they will do the same to you,
To be bigger and better too?

Where's the line between striving for improvement,
and leaving others behind?
Is there a point at which we're too far gone,
to actually stop and look at our lives?
Where we'd rather be rich and alone,
than help someone without a home,
And go flying into the unknown, with our eyes closed.

JACINTA HUDSON

෴

She snuggles in and he keeps her warm.
I can't wait 'til that's me.
The bubbles he blows in her face all swarm.
I can't wait 'til that's me.
She leans over to show something on her phone.
I can't wait 'til that's me.
He reaches out for more chicken, you know.
I can't wait 'til that's me.
She packs up the picnic and stretches with a moan.
The carols are almost over.
It's time to take the family home.
I can't wait until that's me.

Lights are shining. Choirs are singing. Children playing.
This is Christmas.
Picnic baskets line the coast. Families rugged up in warm coats.
For, baby, this is Christmas.
Hugs and kisses shared, as people show they care.
A love like this is rare.
This is Christmas.
Men in shirts. Women in skirts. So, bat your eyes and start to flirt.
'Coz baby, this is Christmas.

JACINTA HUDSON

❧

As shabby as it may be,
I really do love my new tree
It stands out in the unit.
There's something Christmas-y to it.

❧

Violets are blue.
Willows are weepy.
It's time to go to bed now.
Cause I'm just so sleepy.

EMOTIONAL RAMBLINGS

Your poems are good.
Your poems are sweet.
I love the way you make words meet.

I love the way you keep on line.
I love the way you keep in time.
I love the way you make words rhyme.
Look now, I'm stuck,

What rhymes with rhyme?
Each day you tell me something new.
Each day you stop me feeling blue.
You cheer me up. You make me glad.
With you around, I could never be mad.

JACINTA HUDSON

☙❧

The day my joy died; was the day you came alive.
All my pretty pictures, replaced by nasty failures.
There's nothing in my cup, because I can't measure up.
I'm not who I want to be, and it's slowly killing me.

☙❧

I wish I had the words to ease your pain.
I wish that I could find the words to take the ache away.
I wish I had the answers that would make it turn out fine.
I wish there were something more I that could offer,
But all we ever really have is "time".

I want to go back to the way it was
When I had all the say.
I knew what I wanted, and I called all the shots,
And I tackled life in a very different way.

You've given me something I didn't have before.
But you've taken away so much more.
And I don't know who I am now.
I don't know how to be who I am now.

JACINTA HUDSON

They have what I want, and I can't shake the feeling,
That something here is wrong.
Please, someone tell me that I'm dreaming.

I keep praying to higher powers,
But I can see that nothing's changing.
So, I want and pray and wait,
Until the day that I stop aching.

EMOTIONAL RAMBLINGS

❧❧

Shout out to my ladies, who will go to sleep tonight.
Never having had a baby and running out of fight.

Because children make things lighter, they brighten up your world.
Unless you've never had them, so to the darkest depths you swirl.

Your heart will make you dizzy, and your head will lose its mind.
Your soul is dark and heavy, until the light one day you'll find.

JACINTA HUDSON

The breath you just took
Is one they can't catch.
The race you've just run
Is one they can't match.
They're beautiful people
And it's such a shame.
Your ignorance blinds you.
You can't see their pain.
You don't know why they're quiet,
Although they have a lot to say.
You don't know that they say the same thing
Every single day.
Don't judge them, you don't know them
And you haven't walked a mile.
Living with it every day,
Because they don't know another way,
Stronger than you, they smile.

EMOTIONAL RAMBLINGS

※

I can't find my desk and my hot water's gone cold.
This cute little place is in shambles.
The table's a mess and the milk has gone old.
A weird smell fills the air from my candles.

But despite the odd quirks in the space I've been given,
For there's but a few steps to the door,
It's a generous place for which I can live in.
And I couldn't really ask for much more.

JACINTA HUDSON

❦

You walk through the door and all my troubles melt away.
You watch me pace and hear me rant, when you ask about my day.

You're a teddy and a blanket, and an ear to voice my fears.
You're a pillow and a rock, and a shoulder for my fears.

You've all the traits I could've asked for, and some I'd never guess.
You're all I ever wanted, and you never cease to impress.

EMOTIONAL RAMBLINGS

☙❧

It's amazing how you can pick things up,
And go on like you did before.
Just wrap your arms around their waist,
A hug of friendship, nothing more.

It's crazy how bad things can get,
When the ones you want don't want you anymore.
And then how quickly it gets better,
The minute you step through a friend's door.

JACINTA HUDSON

Thank you for the way you smell.
The scent you leave on the pillow that I know so well.
A cross between cigarettes and deodorant.
I love the way it lingers. Almost like you haven't left.

Thank you for the way you look at me.
Like there's something more you're trying to see.
A little mix of intrigue and amazement.
The one that sends shivers all over me.

Thank you for getting it.
For seeing the sense in what doesn't make any.
And somehow understanding that it does.
Because you know that it always has.

Thank you for the time you put in.
And, despite my schedule, never caving.
It's that effort that I can't stop thinking of.
It's part of the new you I've come to love.

❧

Roses are red, violets are blue.
Sugar is sticky, and so is glue.
I'm gonna cover you in sugar,
And then throw you across the room.
You'll get stuck against the wall.
Just like I'm stuck on you.

❧

Believing something different doesn't mean that I am wrong.
Because I walk away doesn't mean that I'm not strong.
I know the tune is odd to you and the lyrics make no sense.
But while you're following footsteps of others,
I'm writing my own song.

JACINTA HUDSON

Chills work through my body, as they try to calm my nerves.
Their job is to rid my brain, of the adrenaline that serves,

To run me into anger or push me away from fear.
It knows not that there's no reason- for, logic it can't hear.

My mind dresses up as my heart, and it sure wears a good disguise.
It tricks me into thinking I'm not, as I repeat again, "I'm fine."

EMOTIONAL RAMBLINGS

~~~

I've all these insecurities playing with my head.
I know I should ignore the voices and listen to my heart instead.

But the past has taught me otherwise,
Small memories create big doubts.
History begins to repeat itself.
And I don't know how to get out.

You fear for my sanity, as you lead me to the ledge.
Pretending that you care for me, you push me closer to the edge.

You piss me off and then wonder, why it is that I am mad at you.
It's really such a pity that you haven't got a clue.

If I take that leap it's people like you who will solely be to blame.
A bright and bubbly girl, destroyed by the world.
Isn't it such a shame?

EMOTIONAL RAMBLINGS

☙❧

Young and sweet and innocent, with a smile upon her face.
For no troubles in this world, have ever touched her grace.

So smart and sweet and beautiful, her hair is light and breezy.
You'd never guess in a million years; she hasn't had it easy.

You think because she smiles at you, she's never had to frown.
You see she's almost always high, so assume she's never down.

You hit her with reality, because you think she's never faced it.
You don't know she's hit it harder, than you could ever make it.

JACINTA HUDSON

One step forward.
Two steps back.
I'm taking too much on and it's tiring.
Three steps forward.
One step back.
If I didn't work so hard, I'd be miserable.
Five steps forward.
Six steps back.
You're worried that I'm getting run down.
Seven steps forward.
Four steps back.
Now I'm five steps ahead.
So you can stop your worrying.

I'd rather be alone than be unhappy.
I'd rather be in pain than be numb.
I'd much rather be stressed than bored.
I'd rather be unemployed
than to have to work for scum.

I'd rather be too rich than be too poor.
And I'd rather be too smart than be too dumb.
But I'd rather have no legs than have no morals.
And I'd rather be independent
that live under another's thumb.

JACINTA HUDSON

❧

You're my inspiration.
A fighter to the end, strong and true.
You're my motivation.
When I'm struggling, I just do as you would do.
So, this is my declaration.
The very best way I could tell you.
That I will follow your direction.
And love you forever, through and through.

Open your eyes and look around.
Try not to be so selfish.
Open your mind, can you hear the sound,
Of those dying at your feet?

Working each day to stay alive,
They claw at their existence.
Oh, such a sight,
their strength and their strive,
To face every challenge they meet.

JACINTA HUDSON

Can you see me? Can you hear me?
Do you understand my pain?
Will you listen? Or is it your mission,
To make me go insane?
Were you present when I told you,
That I see things differently?
Or, off with the fairies, picking daises,
And pretending that you know me?
It seems, I'm screaming for attention.
Just for you to notice me.
And see me as I really am,
Here, in front of you,
Right where I stand.

EMOTIONAL RAMBLINGS

I'll push you out the window.
You'll fall ten thousand feet.
By the time you reach the ground.
You may finally understand.

I'll push you out the window.
Because this is how you treat me.
Such a pity for the rest of us.
You will never understand.

JACINTA HUDSON

❧

A cough for deep breathing.
A smile for some peace.
A laugh for some silence.
A sentence with ease.

Cystic Fibrosis has taken my lungs.
I struggle to move; it hurts to take a breath.
Each inhale and exhale is a war that I'm fighting.
The coughing and wheezing, it all sounds like death.

I am weak; I just want to be strong.
I am skinny, desperate to be a healthy weight.
I'm in hospital, missing out on group activities.
I'm lacking social engagements, every time that I'm away.

Perspective in my mind, understanding in my heart.
But my awesome personality won't make easy of the hard part.
Wishing to be blessed with the things that I am missing.
Instead I am cursed with the things that I don't want.

No cure for such a tragic life.
No choice and no way out.
Transplants are rare, there's no guarantee of air.
A fair trade isn't there and
Tantrums are out of the question,
As you can't even scream and shout.

I take a deep breath.
Then I wheeze, I cough, I splutter.
I whisper, "I'm ok", though it hurts to make a sound.
Mum continues with my physio,
We work together to keep me alive.
The rhythm's almost soothing,
As I listen to her pound.

JACINTA HUDSON

୬୦୧

Roses are lovely and violets are pretty.
It's those without love that I truly do pity.
A sweet and simple blessing bestowed upon the lucky ones.
The kind that go through winter, always looking for the sun.

୬୦୧

Every time I climb a ladder
A snake bites me on the ass.
So, it's time I got the mower out
And butchered all the grass.

❧

The wind would be against me. The rain would be against me.
And I'd be up against a house.
Because when the weather is against me,
That means time is against me.
And let's face it, when you're busy, well isn't that just grouse.

The ladder on uneven ground. The height that I am lacking.
Stressing about the task's importance
Makes me feel like I am cracking.
I can't ask for assistance. I can't pay for the help.
So, do I wait for better weather, or do I do it now myself?

JACINTA HUDSON

I'm worried about you, about her, about him.
I'm worried about this, that, and everything in between.
I'm worried about me, about us, about them.
I'm worried about good, about bad, about sin.

I'm worried about work, about home, and the world.
I'm worried about peace, war, and the arguments that started it all.
I'm worried about how the glass will shatter,
And then scatter all across the floor,
If I don't stop worrying about everything,
And throw the damn thing at the wall.

❧❧

I feel sick to my stomach and I don't know what to think.
Just when I think I've got the answer, my heart begins to sink.
I don't know where friendship ends, and where romance starts.
I don't know how to take a leap, or how to trust my heart.

❧❧

I'm afraid that I'll lose you in a long list of ways,
And you can only see half of them.
You think that all will be fine, and things will unfold with time.
But I'm terrified of how this will end.

JACINTA HUDSON

❧

Years of fighting taught me something.
To never stop looking for that one thing.
The thing that would change your world.
Like nothing else could.

I used to think I'd never find it.
That single one thing that would make my life shift.
Then you changed my world.
Like no one else could.

I feel ever so blessed for the life that I'm living.
And I credit it all to the love that you've given me.
By joining me in my world.
Like no one else could.
And so, changing my world.
Like nothing else could.

EMOTIONAL RAMBLINGS

I'm speechless. I'm breathless. You've stolen my heart.
I feel like I've a lot to say, but don't know where to start.

I've a lot upon my mind, yet I've never been so calm.
I've never felt so close to danger, but completely safe from harm.

I have shivers when it's warm. When it's cool, I'm running hot.
By simply asking for a little, I have somehow gained a lot.

You're the man I've spent years longing for.
And the man I swore I'd find.
And now, in my sights, in my heart and my arms,
I finally have peace of mind.

JACINTA HUDSON

❧

You want all the answers, but I just don't have any.
You want me to see things straight, but I can't find the clarity.
You act like it's so easy, but I can barely breathe.
I require flexibility, but it doesn't come with ease.

❧

There's a hole in my head and the words are leaking out.
Could you stop them for me please as they are fleeing?
Because I'm a writer without words and I just can't figure out.
Who I am without the things that make my being!

❧

Smooth. Rough. Easy. Tough.
Hot. Cold. Subtle. Bold.
Fire. Passion. Peace. Emotion.
Movement. Stillness. Roaring. Silence.

❧

What have I got to fear?
What have I got to lose?
I've got all this support around me.
Except, apparently, from *you*.

JACINTA HUDSON

I want to call you mine.
But I'm not sure where to draw the line.
Can I call you my boyfriend?
Or should I wait and toe the line?
You're sexy and you're talented.
And I want you all the time.
But for now, I'll keep it quiet,
And in my mind, I'll call you mine.

Memories play in my mind.
Your arms around my waist.
Your lips pressed against mine.
They tell the story of our past.
Passion running hot.
Our hands exploring fast.
Reminding me of things I long for.
A lustful hunger. And I want more.

JACINTA HUDSON

※

I can't have me liking you.
Just because you're there.
I can't go on falling,
Because I see your face everywhere.
I need to focus on my life,
And…
What I'm going to wear.
When I'm standing right in front of you,
Breeze blowing through my hair.

EMOTIONAL RAMBLINGS

I don't know what to think or feel.
I'm torn between my fantasies and a need to know what's real.
Logic and emotions fight for a place.
In an over eager heart at the start of a marathon race.
I think I know you pretty well.
But you always keep me guessing, proving I barely know you at all.
I just want to hold your hand.
Knowing I'm safe, feeling calm and able to call you my man.

If only you knew.
The difference it would make.
The way that it would shake us up,
And change but everything.

If only you knew.
The simplest of details.
The way knowing could knock us off the rails,
And send us in the other direction.

If only you knew.
The way I felt back then.
The way I saw things back when we were close,
Much closer than we are now.

If only you knew.
The things that I know.
The things I've yet to tell you,
Of the things I couldn't show.

EMOTIONAL RAMBLINGS

My heart is keeping me down.
I'm sucked in by my gut.
Tangled in intestines.
I'm knee deep in a rut.

I'm trapped within my body.
Fingers claw inside.
My inner voice tries to free itself.
Hoping to get out alive.

JACINTA HUDSON

I love the little curl at the back of your head.
Even when it's messy, after an afternoon in bed.
I love each and every hair on that head.
And I'll never let a soul out there hurt you.

I love those big, blue eyes you have.
So big and bright and bold and innocent.
I love the way they squint when you laugh.
So cheeky and fun and beautiful.

I love how big you are these days.
Even though you're still so small.
I love how big your heart is now.
Still untouched by the hate in this world.

EMOTIONAL RAMBLINGS

☙❧

This is who you are; this is who you've always been.
This is your time to shine, time for you to spread your wings.

You've waited so long for this.
You've worked so hard to get here.
And now your future's ready for you.
Can you feel it calling you?
So close, so near.

Take a deep breath and drink it all in.
I know you can feel it, a new beginning.
This is your moment, your turn, and your time.
This is your baby, your passion and love from deep inside.

When hell takes the form of a circle,
And you can't tell the start from the end.
How can you see the difference,
Between your enemies and your friends?

When the only thing that keeps you sane,
Is the thing that tears you apart.
How do you keep your head on straight,
When the pain numbs the feel of your heart?

EMOTIONAL RAMBLINGS

❦

So, they say you love me.
Where's the proof?
So, they say you care for me.
Show me how.

So, they say you talk to others,
saying just how proud you are of me.
So, tell me now...

When was the last time you told *me*?
When was the last time you held *me* and said that you were proud?
When was the last time you held your tongue,
instead of outright insulting me?

So, they say you love me?
The time to tell me that is *now*.

The hardest years of my life were the ones that I didn't have you.
And the biggest tears to fall from my face,
Were the ones I cried for you.

So, if you're ever looking for evidence to quench the seed of doubt.
All you would need is simply to read,
The pages from years gone without.

For scrawled across those pages is my unconditional love for you.
In every letter of every word, the song of my heart rings true.

❧

Heart don't fail me now.
Give me the courage to see this through.
Feelings find a compromise.
And make my dreams come true.

❧

Congratulations on your news.
A new adventure waits for you.
Congratulations on the little one.
This next adventure will be lots of fun.

JACINTA HUDSON

Tell me that you love me. Tell me that you care.
Tell me that one look at me makes you go crazy;
Makes your mind hazy.
Makes your heart beat faster,
So you can't catch your breath.

Tell me that you're sorry, for the way you've treated me.
And now it's time for us to move forward, to what we should be.
I keep thinking of what we could be.
And it's beautiful.

Can you see them all? The images that play in my head.
A story of a life yet to be lived. Of your holding my hand.
Your arms wrapped around me.
Standing together against the world. Against the cold.

Tell me that you feel it too.
The connection between us.
The fire here within us.
Past and future connects us.
Yet the present seems to elude us.

So, tell me you love me. Show me that you care.

EMOTIONAL RAMBLINGS

૨૦૦૭

Where were you back then?
Where were you back when?
When I was standing right in front of you.
When I was just right, standing in front of you.
Where were you then?

Where were you when I called you friend?
When it didn't matter how the game played out.
As long as we were playing it together.

At what point did you grab a hold of the pen?
And start rewriting how this thing would end.
I thought I knew where we were going.
Until you took us round the bend.

Why couldn't you see me then?
Why couldn't you hear what I'd been saying?
Why wouldn't you listen to the compliments I was paying you?
All the praise I was relaying to you.
All the times I tried to tell you.
I saw more than you could see in you.

Why push me away when you were so near to me?
Why hide the pain and fear from me?
Why wait so long to return to me?
Where were you back then?

JACINTA HUDSON

There's something I want to say.
But I don't know how to put it.
There's a feeling in my heart.
But I don't know where to start.

My family has noticed.
There's a difference to me lately.
I wonder if you see it.
I wonder if you feel the same.

I can't stop talking about you.
Can't get the smile off of my face.
There's a lightness to my aura now.
A sense of newfound grace.

I can't wait to see where this could go.
I can feel a change is coming.
I can't wait to be wrapped up in your arms.
Where, for years, I've longed to be.

The thought of meeting the family.
And all the scary possibilities.
Of what the future could hold for you and me.
Is simply making me crazy.

Picket fences and smoky chimneys.
Crawling infants on bended knees.
Double time and annual leave.
Are all the things that frighten me.

I won't run away or hide from sight.
Rather, I will fight with all my might.
And push past what intimidates me.
To be the woman I've always wanted to be.

JACINTA HUDSON

I hate the way you yell at me.
I hate the way you glare.
I hate the way you roll your eyes.
Like you don't even care.

I hate the way you mock me.
Like you think it doesn't hurt.
I hate the way you treat me.
Like I'm just a piece of dirt.

This isn't the life I imagined.
This isn't the plan I had set.
This wasn't the direction I was taking.
Back before you and I met.

The pictures I see are all strong and confident.
Evidence of bravery I once held true.
But as I stare, I don't recognise the eyes that look back at me.
A year later and I'm someone else- I just wish that I knew who.

JACINTA HUDSON

❧

There's an emptiness inside me,
That I'm not sure how to fill.
Haven't figured out how to do it yet,
But I know, somehow, I will.

❧

Your eyes are so soft, your smile ever so sweet.
And I'm hooked on every word.
A glimpse of a life, I couldn't have dreamed.
And I think you could change my world.

EMOTIONAL RAMBLINGS

I was lost until you found me.
I was drifting, but you bound me.
In your arms tightly wrapped around me.
Now every day you do astound me.

The light in me had surely died.
But when I looked up you were by my side.
And now from you I cannot hide,
The emotions that will not be denied.

JACINTA HUDSON

❦

The darkness is fading, and I can see the light.
All the possibilities of what could be our life.

Like I knew all of the answers, but I didn't know the questions.
Now I've got a little clarity and I'm a little bit more certain.

It's a scary little daydream, and it looks like a lot of work.
But if we tackle it together, it might just have a lot of worth.

EMOTIONAL RAMBLINGS

I've got a picture in my mind, of how my life should be.
It hasn't changed for years now.
It's been the same since I was three.

But the puzzle isn't working out, and the picture isn't clear.
There are pieces that are missing, and some that shouldn't be here.

But I don't know how to fix it, or how to make it right.
I know it won't be easy, and I'm not sure if it's worth the fight.

I know the right words to say.
But I can't seem to put them in sentences.
I know the right games to play.
But I can't seem to work out the rules.

I've all the right pieces to work with.
But the puzzle still won't come together.
I've got maps to show me the way.
But I've still no idea where I'm going.

Heart and head at war with each other.
I don't know right from wrong.
I want to be impulsive, want to take another.
But I don't know who I am.

Black and white on the surface.
But its grey all in-between.
Colours keep on blurring.
Contradictions keep on showing.
And I don't know who to be.

JACINTA HUDSON

You know you can't mess me up.
You can push me down
But I'll get back up.

Because you know I'm tough enough.
So, you can push all you want,
Because this fight ain't over 'til I say it's over.
You can push and prod and knock me over.

But I ain't staying down.
This fight ain't over 'til I say it's over.

Listen here, I'm talking to you.
Let me make this clear.
Let me get this through.
There ain't anything in this world that you can do.
Nothing you can throw at me that I won't catch.
No challenge that you can pose that I won't match.

Listen up, this is how it's going to go.
I make the rules here and there's something you should know.
Quit while you're ahead.
Because you're never going to win.
Your streak of crap is done here, this is the end.
This is my time to shine.
This is where my reign begins.

JACINTA HUDSON

Stop procrastinating.
Stop wasting all your time.
Stop scribbling and jotting down,
The thoughts that fill your mind.

Stop putting off what you need to do.
Just suck it up and do it.
Stop ignoring what is good for you.
Just pick something and go for it.

I feel like I'm not me.
Like I'm floating up above or sitting here beside me.
I feel like I'm not right.
Like I can see the things I want, but what I want is out of sight.
I feel like I can't reach myself.
Like I can't touch the things I need. I'm out of touch with myself.
I feel like something's missing.
A hole inside. A life un-lived.
A book not read. And I don't know where to start.

JACINTA HUDSON

❦

All these words are circling in my head.
No sense can be made of them, they don't go together.
Sentences all mix and match.
Up and down. Cross the latch.
Back and forth, over the latter, around the former,
And coming to an abrupt halt, just before the end.
The madness from this sanity.
The sense from crazy ramblings.
Shingles and sixpence in a world of grilled cheese sandwiches.

❦

Tweeddale Dee and Tweeddale Dum
Are playing with their Pokémon.
Tweeddale Dee shouts out "I won!"
And so, does Tweeddale Dum.

In the quiet of the night
    In a quiet little town
        Of a quiet little area
            Was a woman gone wild.
With her wild, bright eyes
    And her wild, curly hair
        She took her wild, edgy attitude
            And painted the town.
In shades of red and black
    She took her fabric scissors
        Never flawed by paper
            To tear apart the town.
Shreds of iron and timber
    Were strewn across the road
        As she tore apart the buildings
            And then drove off all alone.

JACINTA HUDSON

It kills me that I miss you.
I'm trying to get over it. I'm trying to move on.
But even so, I miss you. You'll always be in my heart.
It bugs me that I can't be with you.
The voice keeps saying we're meant to be.
All the same, I can't be with you. I'll still love you anyway.
It annoys me that you won't talk to me.
I'll never get the answers I'm looking for.
Either way, it won't make a difference.
I guess some things never change.
It drives me nuts that I can't get over you.
Even after all this time.

I can't do this.
I can't pretend.
Like everything is fine.
When I'm clearly going round the bend.

When my tears betray me.
When my heart just wants to fly.
When sense and reason take a hit.
And my mind would rather die.

JACINTA HUDSON

❧

Why are you so cruel?
Do you really have nothing better to do,
Than to insult me, every chance you get?

Am I a person to you?
Or more like a pet?
Kicking me while I'm down.
Pushing me around.

Don't go playing innocent.
We know you do it on purpose.
How else can you bring my insecurities to the surface?
When usually I hide them so well,
Somewhere you can't see,
And that's why you don't know the real me.

Because I'm too scared to show you,
And be made to look the fool.
You make me feel like such a tool,
To like the things I do.
Just because I'm not like you.
Such a shame, that I have to play your game, and hide away,
Or face the tears for one more day.

EMOTIONAL RAMBLINGS

൞

Everyone's so set against it. The first thing I've wanted in years.
They all think that I'm crazy. Their opinions bring me to tears.

They don't know what it's like to love you.
There's no way that they'll understand.
Most of them have never even met you.
They can't see why I want you around.

Holding on is killing me. But letting go won't change a thing.
My friends and family try to help.
But their words aren't helping, only hurting.

I've tried to analyse it all. I've tried to let it go.
I've tried to give you time and space.
I've tried letting my love and pain show.

But nothing seems to make a difference.
Nothing seems to be working.
Unable to change the pain. Unable to fill the void.
Unable to think of anything but your arms, your face, your voice.

I'm stuck in a rut and can't go on.
I'm stuck in a loop that won't end.
I'm stuck on you, and somehow that's wrong.
With you, I'm whole and I'm broken, unable to mend.

JACINTA HUDSON

Wonderful buildings that rise to the sky.
Skiing from mountain tops, ever so high.
From hotel to hotel, a new night a new town.
We'll take in the sights from all around.

New foods to try and new places to go.
Streets filled with art and music that flows.
For glorious fiestas try not to be late.
With all of this culture I know I can't wait.

One day I'll walk down an isle of white,
in a beautiful sparkling dress.
I'll greet my bridesmaids before turning to face
the man that I've dressed to impress.

In front of a crowd of my friends and my family,
I will vow to forever be his.
Then we'll both say, "I do" and the ceremony will end,
with a wonderful movie like kiss.

JACINTA HUDSON

Three dollars a day and you sleep under your machine.
You've a family of five and five dollars in the bank.
You fight for your family and for freedom you'll flee.
Your best friend is dying and there's no water in the tank.

We're watching the world slowly rot away in pieces.
The roses bloom in winter because the weather has gone mad.
We say that we care but the reality of this is.
We're all awake with our eyes closed and it really is quite sad.

To my left, he needs some money, to my right, she needs a meal.
But you know I'm bound to spend my cash
on dinner with my friends.
It shouldn't be so hard for us to see the bigger deal.
So, can somebody tell me, when this agony will end.

You're selfish and sadistic. You're cruel and you don't care.
You're full of good excuses. You bullshit through your point.
Your abuse comes in so many forms. It's hard to keep up.
Will you throw me against a wall today?
Or just make me feel insane?

Defensive when I call you on it. I'm just over-reacting.
So, I stay silent the next time- and now I'm in a "bitchy" mood.
I can never win with you. What do you want from me?
I have yet to scream and swear and slam your head into the table.
Would that be better? Should I try that next?

You don't see the problem. I see it all unfolding.
You're acting just like he did- and we all know how that ended.
One day there'll be a gap between us. A canyon of hurt and pain.
But then, you always think I'm wrong, so maybe, then again.

You're not selfish or sadistic.
And of course, I know you care.
Because I'm a bitch and you're an angel.
Somehow that doesn't seem fair.

JACINTA HUDSON

❧

There are so few words to describe how I feel.
Finally, you can begin to heel.
From all the years of pain and despair.
Now that your little one is finally here.

Wrapped in your arms so snug and tight.
Thanks to the years you continued to fight.
For a love you knew would be yours in the end.
So now there's no need for you to pretend.

Gorgeous angelic baby smiles abound.
There's no greater love in the world to be found.
And I'm so beyond happy you can close those old doors.
And open the one where this angel is yours.

Beyond belief is the strength you have shown.
To see a day when you could hold your own.
It may feel like a dream, but I promise it's true.
And no one deserves this more than you do.

EMOTIONAL RAMBLINGS

❧

The race to get you here.
The fight to keep you near.
When the bright light shines upon us.
It will highlight what is clear.

The war I won't surrender.
The struggle I will push through.
The knowledge in my heart and soul.
That I'd give anything for you.

❧

You're there for me when no one else is.
You're always generous and never selfish.
You're my heart, my mind and my very soul.
For every moment I keep you close,
is a moment you keep me whole.

JACINTA HUDSON

Every time you push me, I fall.
To get back on my feet, I must crawl.
You anticipate my move before I make it.
Before I piece together my spirit, you break it.

It's a tug of war that I'm losing.
It's a life or death option I'm choosing.
Every time I make a choice you change my mind.
It's the clarity I'm looking for that I can't find.

You're right when I'm wrong and it's confusing.
Then, something occurs to me as I am musing.
You're the opposite of all that I'm thinking.
I'm fighting myself and I'm sinking.

I don't usually say this, but there's something you should know.
While I'm keeping quiet, there's something I don't show.
You seem to think you know me; I must tell you that you're wrong.
I appear to be quite fragile, but I'm really very strong.
It occurs to me that you can't see this, as it does that you are thick.
So, let me break it down for you, you selfish, arrogant dick.

I say yes when I mean no, just so you think that I agree with you.
I will do exactly what I'm told, and you won't hear me complain.
I can put up with your anger, even though I shouldn't have to.
And I'll pretend as though I'm happy to make you feel ok.

But please remember for me, this tiny little detail.
I'm not your slave and I don't work for you,
You pathetic little male.

JACINTA HUDSON

You push me and you prod me and knock me all around.
You tease me and you taunt me and then kick me to the ground.
You make a fuss about everything and I don't make a sound.
And after years of bullying, this is what I've found...

If I keep quiet, then I'm weak
If I speak up, then I'm too loud.
By trying to defend myself
And put you in your place, I'm too proud.

But there's something that I've noticed,
Something I know that you can't see.
While you're afraid to be yourself,
I'm ok with being me.

The warmth in your smile. The love in your touch.
Your advice about life, I'll miss ever so much.
Your time and your care. Your heart and your soul.
When all my pieces broke apart,
you were the one that made me whole.

~

Find some peace within you,
Find the peace within your soul.
Find the you that's truthful,
And then you'll find the you that's whole.

JACINTA HUDSON

You make my heart sing; you make my soul soar.
You make me feel like no one has done before.
You make my life better in so many ways.
And maybe if I'm lucky, forever you will stay.

EMOTIONAL RAMBLINGS

ABOUT THE AUTHOR

Jacinta is the author of poetry books, Just a Thought and Emotional Ramblings. Residing in Victoria, Australia, she is a new mother, learning to juggle parenting with her love of writing. She has a blog, on her website, where she shares her experiences as a "newbie" writer and her advice to those who feel the same.

CONNECT WITH JACINTA

www.jacintahudson.com
www.instagram.com/jacintahudson
www.facebook.com/JacintaHudsonWriting

JACINTA HUDSON

www.ingramcontent.com/pod-product-compliance
Lightning Source LLC
Chambersburg PA
CBHW070256010526
44107CB00056B/2479